essential careers™

CAREERS IN
METEOROLOGY

CORONA BREZINA

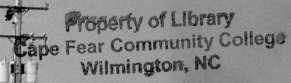

ROSEN
PUBLISHING

NEW YORK

Published in 2013 by The Rosen Publishing Group, Inc.
29 East 21st Street, New York, NY 10010

First Edition

Library of Congress Cataloging-in-Publication Data

Brezina, Corona.
Careers in meteorology/Corona Brezina.—1st ed.
   p. cm.—(Essential careers)
Includes bibliographical references and index.
ISBN 978-1-4488-8241-0 (lib. bdg.)
1. Meteorology—Vocational guidance—Juvenile literature. 2. Meteorologists—
Juvenile literature. I. Title.
QC869.5.B74 2013
551.5023—dc23

2012012557

Manufactured in the United States of America

CPSIA Compliance Information: Batch #W13YA: For further information, contact Rosen Publishing, New York, New York, at 1-800-237-9932.

contents

INTRO

Weather Channel meteorologist Jim Cantore reports on the onslaught of Hurricane Irene, in August of 2011, from Battery Park in New York City, which experienced flooding during the storm.

DUCTION

Meteorology is the science of the atmosphere, the envelope of gases surrounding Earth. Meteorologists study the forces in the atmosphere that shape weather and climate. Many meteorologists are forecast meteorologists, who analyze weather data and issue predictions using sophisticated computer models, as well as their own experience and expertise. Other meteorologists conduct research, monitor air quality, teach, and, of course, present the forecast on television.

Meteorology is one of those fields in which people can make a great career out of doing something they love. Tracking and studying the weather can be endlessly fascinating. Pursuing meteorology as a career means learning to understand and predict the forces behind weather and climate phenomena. Meteorology is not an easy profession, however. It requires a college degree heavy on science and math. Weather forecasters may be required to work irregular hours, especially during severe weather events. The job can entail tight and stressful deadlines and a taxing workload.

Nevertheless, most meteorologists love their jobs and embrace the challenges. In 2011, the director of the National Weather Service (NWS), Dr. John L. Hayes, told an interviewer, "Think about the awesome power and mystery of the atmosphere and the elements out there and being able to deliver forecasts to fundamentally protect life and property. What can be more fulfilling than that?"

Weather affects our daily lives, our health, and our recreational pursuits. It has far-reaching economic consequences, as

A scientist at the National Hurricane Center examines data on the 2011 storm season, which saw twenty tropical storms, including four major hurricanes.

well. Weather disasters can cause billions of dollars in damage. Economic sectors such as agriculture, construction, and transportation are all highly dependent on the weather and on accurate weather forecasts. Many industries in these areas employ meteorologists for advice on how to plan for upcoming weather. An expanding private sector accounts for much of the

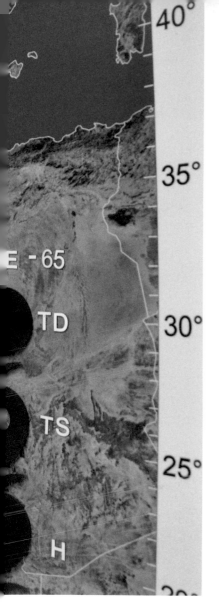

job growth in the field. Meteorologists work for utility companies, airlines, insurance companies, recreational businesses, and private consulting firms. The biggest employer of meteorologists is the government, and the number of meteorologists working for the government is expected to remain steady.

The Bureau of Labor Statistics (BLS) predicts that job growth in the field-of-meteorology will grow at a faster than average rate between 2008 and 2018. During this period, employment is expected to increase by about 15 percent. Competition for job openings, however, is expected to be keen. In general, meteorology jobs pay well. Up-to-date salary figures can be found in the BLS' *Occupational Outlook Handbook*.

chapter 1

PREPARING FOR A
CAREER IN METEOROLOGY

Are you an aspiring meteorologist? The pathway to a meteorology career begins with a keen interest in the weather, a fascination that makes you want to learn about the scientific principles behind thunderstorms and the wind chill factor. Your interest, however, must take you away from the sun and rain and into studies of science, math, and computers, which are essential to a meteorologist's education. Then you must step back and appreciate the wide range of applications of meteorology.

Meteorologists are known mostly as weather forecasters, but atmospheric science encompasses a huge range of weather and climate topics. You might be drawn to the wild side, with hurricanes and tornadoes; the dirty side, where you study how pollution affects the atmosphere and environment; or the extreme side, where you study droughts, floods, and climate change. Meteorology also has a pragmatic side—meteorologists often apply their knowledge to fields such as agriculture, transportation, renewable energy, and defense. There is even a theoretical side, where meteorologists study topics such as the composition of the atmosphere and the physics behind hurricanes.

HIGH SCHOOL

A solid background for meteorology begins with plenty of high school coursework in science, math, and computers. Students should take advantage of every science class available, including chemistry, physics, and earth sciences. Knowledge of a foreign language can also be useful. Students should develop good communication skills, both verbal and written.

Extracurricular activities might offer opportunities to explore meteorology further. Some schools have science or weather clubs, or offer participation in science activities such as Science Olympics or science fairs. A school may issue weather broadcasts on the radio or weather alerts on its Web site, and students might be able to volunteer their help in these efforts.

School activities such as science fair projects offer a good opportunity for independent study on topics that are related to meteorology, such as the carbon cycle.

Many National Weather Service forecast offices offer tours in which people can see the instruments, operations area, and communications center. TV broadcast meteorologists often make public appearances as well. Check out the TV station's Web page for possible chances to meet your local forecaster, and take a look at any other weather-related resources the site might offer.

ARMED FORCES

There are many reasons why a high school student might consider military service after graduation. People join the military to achieve personal discipline, prove their worth, and serve their country. Service offers an opportunity to travel, provides good benefits, and guarantees a job. It also offers superb educational and on-the-job-training opportunities. The Reserve Officers' Training Corps (ROTC) program offers college tuition scholarships for students who commit to military service after graduation and participate in some training sessions during the school year. High school students who are certain of their future plans may be able to participate in junior ROTC.

Military service provides training in a variety of job fields, including meteorology. The air force and the navy both operate sophisticated weather facilities. A meteorologist who receives training through the military will acquire considerable experience in making forecasts and in other areas of meteorology. This will ensure good job prospects upon return to civilian life, while also paving the way for a lifelong career within the military if desired.

ASSOCIATE DEGREES AND APPRENTICESHIPS

Another option upon graduation is to pursue a two-year associate degree at a technical college or community college.

STUDYING TO BE A CERTIFIED BROADCAST METEOROLOGIST

The American Meteorological Society (AMS) established its certified broadcast meteorologist program to raise the professional standards for broadcast meteorologists. To be certified, broadcast meteorologists must show that they meet the educational and experience criteria by passing a test of their knowledge of meteorology and related sciences and their ability to communicate information to the public in an accessible manner.

The test is made up of one hundred multiple-choice and true-or-false questions. They cover a broad range of fifteen topics, including severe storm structure, flooding, thermodynamics, regional weather, data and instruments, and climatology and climate change. To be certified, applicants have to pass with a score of 75 percent or higher and fulfill the remaining certification requirements. Prospective broadcast meteorologists have three chances to pass the test, and those who do not pass in three tries can make another attempt after a yearlong wait.

The AMS does not provide sample test questions, but it does provide an online study guide, which can be viewed at http://www.ametsoc.org/amscert/cbmstudyguide.html. The guide provides links to materials provided by the National Oceanic and Atmospheric Administration (NOAA) and university meteorology programs. There are also links to free study modules offered by the Cooperative Program for Operational Meteorology, Education, and Training (COMET).

In general, meteorology jobs require a four-year degree. Nonetheless, many community colleges offer a few basic courses in meteorology, and some community colleges have good meteorology programs. A community college student who decides to pursue meteorology as a career may eventually decide to transfer to a four-year college to finish a bachelor's degree.

Community colleges and technical colleges offer programs in instrumentation technology, electronics, and engineering. A degree in any of these areas qualifies graduates to work as meteorological equipment technicians who install, service, and repair meteorological instruments, from nephoscopes (instruments that measure the movement of clouds) to radar systems. Coursework in meteorology will also give equipment technicians a good background for the job.

Some community colleges and other institutions also offer apprenticeship programs in instrumentation technology and related areas. Apprenticeships generally combine classroom instruction with hands-on training.

A BACHELOR'S DEGREE AND BEYOND

Most meteorologists hold at least an undergraduate degree in meteorology, atmospheric science, or a related major. Meteorology is a demanding major, but taking the

time to study and earn good grades will pay off in the long run. A student interested in eventually pursuing graduate studies in meteorology may start out by earning an undergraduate degree in chemistry, physics, computer science, or math. Proficiency

Atmospheric science is related to a variety of other sciences. Astronomy, for example, helps a meteorologist understand factors such as how the position and angle of the sun affect weather.

in a couple of different computer languages will be a valuable skill on the job for any meteorologist.

In choosing a college or university, take a close look at the specific departments and programs. Choose a program that is strong in your preferred area, whether it's broadcast meteorology, research, or some other focus. You might also want to take classes in related sciences, such as oceanography, climatology, or astronomy. Consider a second major or minor that will complement a meteorology or atmospheric science major. If you plan to work in broadcast meteorology, take communications courses and participate in college television and radio. If you hope to be a high-level manager or start your own company, take business courses. If your dream is to draft environmental policy, take classes in government or economics.

A master's or doctorate degree is necessary for careers in research and for many higher-level meteorology jobs. When applying for jobs, additional academic credentials and advanced degrees will give you an edge over other candidates who hold just a bachelor's degree.

Be sure to apply for financial aid for undergraduate study. The American Meteorological Society (AMS) offers scholarships, including a minority scholarship aimed at encouraging traditionally underrepresented groups to pursue atmospheric or a related science. Financial aid is generally not available for graduate study programs, but students can apply for fellowships, conduct research, or work as a teaching assistant to help pay for school. These arrangements also provide work experience that will look good on a résumé.

CAREER PREPARATION

As you're working your way through college and, perhaps, graduate school, keep a lookout for internships, student jobs, and other programs that will give you hands-on opportunities in the field and enhance your résumé. The National Weather Service offers a number of different employment opportunities for students and runs an unpaid volunteer service program. Various other government departments also employ interns, and many TV stations and other media outlets hire interns who have an interest in meteorology.

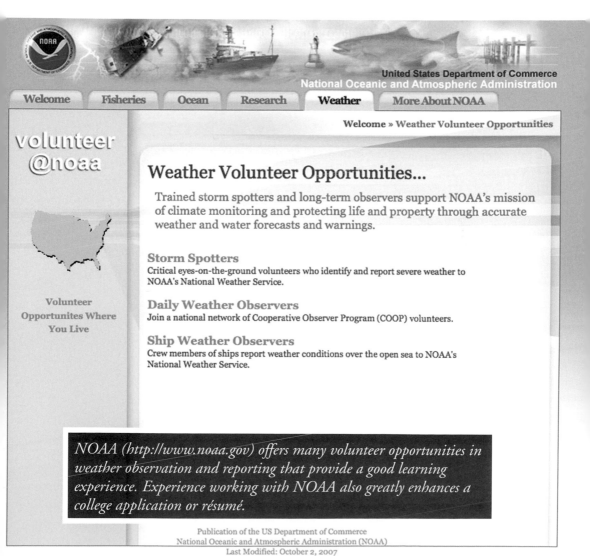

United States Department of Commerce
National Oceanic and Atmospheric Administration

Welcome   Fisheries   Ocean   Research   **Weather**   More About NOAA

Welcome » Weather Volunteer Opportunities

volunteer @noaa

Volunteer Opportunites Where You Live

Weather Volunteer Opportunities...

Trained storm spotters and long-term observers support NOAA's mission of climate monitoring and protecting life and property through accurate weather and water forecasts and warnings.

Storm Spotters
Critical eyes-on-the-ground volunteers who identify and report severe weather to NOAA's National Weather Service.

Daily Weather Observers
Join a national network of Cooperative Observer Program (COOP) volunteers.

Ship Weather Observers
Crew members of ships report weather conditions over the open sea to NOAA's National Weather Service.

NOAA (http://www.noaa.gov) offers many volunteer opportunities in weather observation and reporting that provide a good learning experience. Experience working with NOAA also greatly enhances a college application or résumé.

Publication of the US Department of Commerce
National Oceanic and Atmospheric Administration (NOAA)
Last Modified: October 2, 2007
Contact: christopher.vaccaro@noaa.gov

One unique opportunity open to meteorology students during the summer is Significant Opportunities in Atmospheric Research and Science (SOARS) at the National Center for Atmospheric Research (NCAR). The program particularly encourages participation of minority groups. Students spend ten weeks conducting research supported by mentors.

An internship is the first level of employment with the NWS. Interns often rotate among a few different weather forecast offices, where they experience different types of regional weather patterns, before receiving permanent placement. They become familiar with NWS instruments and procedures during this training period.

chapter 2

CAREERS AT THE NWS AND NOAA

The U.S. government is the largest employer of meteorologists. It employs about one-third of all meteorologists nationwide. Among these, the greatest number work for the National Weather Service and other branches of the National Oceanic and Atmospheric Administration, which is the government agency devoted to weather, climate, oceans, and atmosphere. The NOAA collaborates with other government agencies, as well as with private and academic organizations.

The NOAA is a division of the Department of Commerce, the federal cabinet office that promotes economic growth by supporting business and communities. This reflects the importance of the NOAA's role in providing vital information and services that impact the national economy and people's everyday lives. Business enterprises in sectors from transportation to agriculture make decisions based on the NOAA's weather and climate predictions. Industries, communities, and individuals all rely on the NOAA to issue emergency alerts for extreme weather events, such as dangerous storms, hurricanes, and tornadoes. Meteorologists employed by the NOAA can feel pride that their mission is to protect the public, support economic stability, and help preserve natural resources.

The NOAA employs meteorologists and specialists in related fields to work in a variety of capacities. Most people are probably familiar with meteorologists primarily as forecasters. Weather forecasting is at the heart of the field of meteorology, but forecast meteorologists are backed up by a global support network. A forecast meteorologist—also called an operational meteorologist—draws on data from weather stations across the country.

A meteorologist at the National Hurricane Center tracks the progress of a hurricane using computer models that predict its direction, wind speed, and strength.

Other sources of weather data used to create a forecast include weather buoys in bodies of water, weather balloons, radar systems, and satellites orbiting Earth. Other meteorologists analyze all of this data and develop computer models to generate more accurate predictions.

Some meteorologists are involved in research work to improve the scientific understanding of weather. They, too, are supported by engineers and technicians who develop, install, and service instruments and computer software.

THE NATIONAL WEATHER SERVICE (NWS)

The NWS employs about five thousand people, the greatest number of them highly trained meteorologists. It has its headquarters in Silver Spring, Maryland, with 6 regional offices and 122 weather forecast offices across the country. In addition, twenty-one Center Weather Service Units tailor forecasts specifically for aircraft operations, monitoring conditions such as thunderstorms, turbulence, and precipitation. There are also thirteen River Forecast Centers that issue river and flood forecasts and monitor the water supply.

PROFILE: JOHN L. HAYES, NWS DIRECTOR

Appointed in 2007, Dr. John L. Hayes is the National Weather Service director and the National Oceanic and Atmospheric Administration assistant administrator for weather services. Hayes started out by earning a bachelor's degree in mathematics from Bowling Green University. He went on to receive doctorate and master's degrees from the Naval Post Graduate School. During an eighteen-year career in the air force, Hayes attained the rank of colonel and rose to become commander of the Air Force Weather Agency.

After retiring from the military in 1998, Hayes managed the Automated Weather Interactive Processing System (AWIPS) program at Litton-PRC, a private company, through 2000. He then held a number of high-level positions for the NOAA in which he oversaw research programs, emergency response, and science and technology. Before being appointed NWS director, Hayes served as director of the World Weather Watch Department at the World Meteorological Organization (WMO), a specialized agency of the United Nations (UN).

Each weather forecast office typically includes a meteorologist-in-charge, a warning coordination meteorologist, five senior forecasters, three to five journeyman forecasters, and various other interns, officers, analysts, technicians, and administrative staff members. The office issues two to four forecasts daily and keeps the public informed of any severe weather watches or warnings. NWS offices also issue specialized information, such as fire or aviation forecasts.

Forecasts are based on data from millions of observations taken daily from various sources, including satellites, radars, weather balloons, aircraft, ships, and observation stations, many of them automated. Over one thousand of these stations, mostly located at airports, issue frequent observations on temperature and dew point, wind speed and direction, barometric pressure, precipitation, and sky conditions. In addition, volunteer observers across the country take daily measurements.

All of this incoming data is collected, collated, and used to create computer models that predict the movements of the atmosphere. Meteorologists use these models, raw data, and knowledge of weather systems to generate a forecast. Staff at each weather forecast office are familiar with the weather patterns typical of their specific geographic area.

NATIONAL CENTERS FOR ENVIRONMENTAL PREDICTION (NCEP)

The NWS also includes the National Centers for Environmental Prediction (NCEP), specialized centers that focus on specific weather and climate subject areas. Some, such as the Storm Prediction Center and the National Hurricane Center, are familiar to the public. Others, such as the Environmental Modeling Center, are not as well known but provide valuable services. The meteorologists and other experts at the centers provide detailed, pertinent, and timely information in their area of expertise. They also conduct research and develop tools and products that improve forecasting and guidance.

The NCEP is made up of nine centers:
- The Aviation Weather Center provides warnings and forecasts relevant to aircraft.
- The Climate Prediction Center monitors and forecasts short-term (under one year) climate events.
- The Environmental Modeling Center works to develop and improve weather, ocean, and climate model and analysis systems.
- The Hydrometeorological Prediction Center issues forecasts and analyses on weather events involving heavy amounts of precipitation.

- NCEP Central Operations supports the other centers and distributes forecasts and tools.
- The National Hurricane Center forecasts the movement of hurricanes and tropical storms and issues watches and warnings to affected areas.
- The Ocean Prediction Center issues warnings and forecasts for weather in the Atlantic and Pacific.
- The Space Weather Prediction Center issues alerts and warnings for space weather events, such as solar flares, that can affect Earth's atmosphere.
- The Storm Prediction Center issues watches and warnings for thunderstorms, tornadoes, and other severe weather across the United States.

Most of the centers are located in Camp Springs, Maryland, with four exceptions. The Aviation Camp Center is located in Kansas City, Missouri, the Storm Prediction Center in Norman, Oklahoma, the Space Weather Prediction Center in Boulder, Colorado, and the National Hurricane Center in Miami, Florida.

JOB REQUIREMENTS AND COMPENSATION

Most meteorology positions require at least an undergraduate degree with a relevant major, such as meteorology or atmospheric sci-ence. The NWS, for example, requires twenty-four semester hours in courses related to meteorology, plus nine semester hours in such areas as related physical sciences, computer science, or

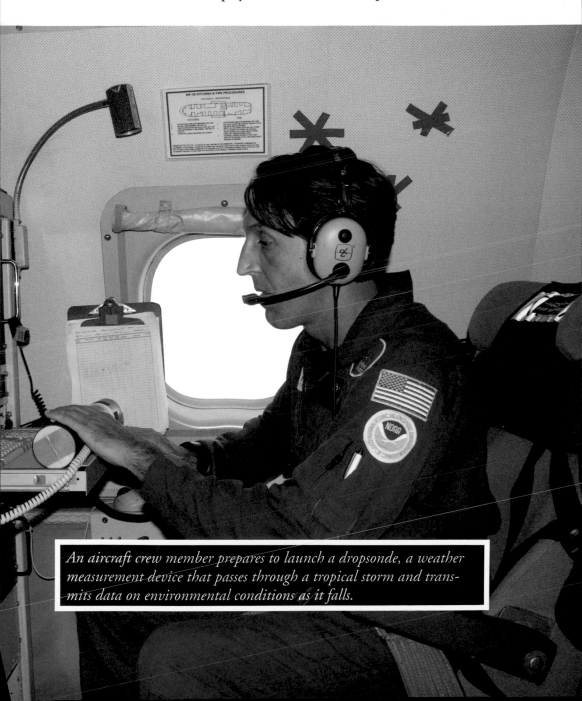

An aircraft crew member prepares to launch a dropsonde, a weather measurement device that passes through a tropical storm and trans-mits data on environmental conditions as it falls.

A meteorologist takes a reading at a meteorological measuring station. The screen enclosures protect instruments from the elements and ensure standardized measurements among stations.

math. Higher positions often require a master's degree, and many meteorologists pursue a doctorate.

A NWS meteorologist must have solid skills in time management and be able to work under pressure. The job requires analytical thinking, attention to detail, and good organization. In addition, a NWS meteorologist must have excellent communication skills. The job may involve communicating with colleagues in other federal, state, and local agencies, as well as with the media and the public. Good communication skills can be crucial during extreme weather situations. Such events may require clear communication with Federal Emergency Management Agency (FEMA) personnel and journalists covering a big story, not to mention members of the public whose safety may depend upon a clear and comprehensible storm warning.

Job seekers applying for employment with the federal government use the Web site USAJobs.com, which lists nearly all of the open positions in every government department. Federal employees are paid according to a fixed general schedule (GS), which ranks the pay rate into fifteen different grades. Entry-level jobs generally fall into the lower grades. New entrants into the workforce often start out as interns. A recent college graduate may begin at a GS-5 pay level, before eventually being promoted to higher and better-paying positions. Top-level management positions receive the GS-15 pay rate, the highest level in the schedule.

Some government departments, including the NOAA, offer temporary student employment and unpaid volunteer service for students. Even though they don't pay well—or at all—these programs offer an excellent opportunity for work experience and training.

Meteorological agencies monitor the weather 24 hours a day, 7 days a week, 365 days a year. A career in meteorology, both in the public (government) and private sectors, often requires working some weekends, nights, and holidays. NWS employees, for example, work on a rotating shift schedule. Extreme weather events may also entail overtime work. Depending on specific duties, meteorologists may have to travel or spend time outdoors doing fieldwork. Employees for some NOAA divisions spend extended periods of time aboard ships monitoring conditions on the ocean.

Yet government jobs also offer generous benefits and time off. This includes medical insurance, life insurance, a retirement plan, ten paid holidays, and two weeks' vacation time in the first year of employment.

chapter 3

OTHER GOVERNMENT METEOROLOGY CAREERS

E very year, natural disasters cause tens or even hundreds of billions of dollars worth of damage worldwide. Extreme weather events, such as hurricanes and floods, are a significant contributor to these losses. In addition, smaller losses caused by weather can quickly add up. A drought can be devastating to a farmer, but a year with rainfall just slightly below average can also hurt profits substantially. A major snowstorm brings aviation traffic to a standstill, but a dense fog can also lead to canceled or delayed flights.

Government departments turn to meteorologists and their expertise to anticipate the impact of weather events and minimize the resulting damages and harm. Many government departments work in cooperation with the National Weather Service. Some departments also run their own weather programs that provide specialized forecasts. Advances in technology have made it possible to generate a much more detailed and focused forecast than in the past.

U.S. MILITARY

The U.S. Department of Defense (DOD) operates a number of weather programs that support military operations, missions, and day-to-day functioning around the world. In some cases, military meteorologists take observations and make forecasts in places where there is no conventional observation equipment available. In other cases, meteorological observations might involve specialized capabilities unique to military requirements.

The Air Force Weather Agency (AFWA) is one of the leading DOD weather-related programs. The agency provides weather forecasts, analyses, and aircrew mission briefings to military installations across the United States. It also tracks global environmental intelligence and keeps command informed. Global environmental intelligence includes ground and climate conditions as well as conditions in space—the air force maintains four solar observatories. The AFWA also works on developing cutting-edge weather technologies.

The meteorological function of the U. S. Navy's Meteorology and Oceanography Comand program focuses on marine weather forecasting. Navy meteorologists and other experts

In 2011, the aftermath of Hurricane Irene caused record flooding in Paterson, New Jersey, as rivers overflowed and left homes and roads underwater.

also issue aviation forecasts and communicate weather advisories and environmental conditions to ships and helicopters.

The DOD also operates the Defense Meteorological Satellite Program (DMSP), a system of satellites that gather meteorological data that is shared with civilian agencies. In addition, the army and marine corps maintain smaller weather programs.

OTHER GOVERNMENT DEPARTMENTS

Many other federal agencies hire meteorologists to issue forecasts and conduct research. State and local governments may also be in need of meteorologists. Historically, the National Aeronautics and Space Administration (NASA) has been a pioneer and innovator in weather research and technological developments. Manned space shuttle launches required that there be no chance of bad weather on liftoff days—and no room for error in meteorologists' forecasts. Today, despite the end of the shuttle program, NASA still conducts weather research and launches satellites. Instruments on NASA's satellites track observations on Earth's land, oceans, and atmosphere. Specific topics within NASA's many research areas include atmospheric composition, precipitation, and hurricane data. NASA partners with the NOAA and many other scientific agencies and organizations.

The Department of Energy (DOE) also employs meteorologists and atmospheric scientists, largely in research positions. A clear understanding of weather patterns is critical to energy security, especially regarding renewable resources such as solar and wind energy. The DOE operates an Office of Science and runs seventeen research labs across the country, some of which offer opportunities in atmospheric research.

DIY FORECASTING

Weather enthusiasts who want to gain some hands-on familiarity with research, data collection, record keeping, and forecasting can easily set up a basic weather station. The first step is setting up instruments that will measure temperature, atmospheric pressure, humidity, precipitation, and wind speed and direction. The barometer, which measures air pressure, should be kept indoors away from any air vents. The thermometer and hygrometer, which measures humidity, should be kept in a sheltered area outdoors, well out of the sun. A rain gauge should be positioned a good distance away from buildings and trees. The wind vane and anemometer, an instrument that measures wind speed, should be installed high up but not near or on top of buildings.

Every day at the same time, or twice a day, if possible, check the instruments and record your findings. Take note of any observations, such as clear skies, fog, or lightning nearby. Use your data to spot weather patterns and trends and make a prediction about upcoming weather. Over time, you'll be astonished to discover how attuned you can become to the weather around you.

The Environmental Protection Agency (EPA) is the federal department charged with protecting human health and the environment. The EPA employs meteorologists and atmospheric scientists who track and study various aspects of weather and climate. An EPA meteorologist may devise strategies for controlling air pollution, develop new weather models, or study how climate change affects natural resources. The EPA has offices across the country and also conducts research at a number of laboratories. EPA meteorologists and atmospheric scientists are involved in drafting environmental policy and regulations.

The U.S. Department of Agriculture (USDA) is another government department with significant interest in the weather. Fluctuations in weather can dramatically impact crop production and, therefore, future food supplies and prices. The USDA, along with the NOAA, operates the Joint Agricultural Weather Facility (JAWF), which monitors weather and assesses the effects of weather on crops worldwide. The USDA also operates the Natural Resources Conservation Service (NRCS). The NRCS focuses on agricultural land and water supplies, but it also addresses climate issues, air quality, and weather.

In addition to those federal offices already mentioned, many other government departments also hire meteorologists. A selection of these include the Bureau of Land Management, the Bureau of Reclamation, the National Science Foundation, the Occupational Safety and Health Administration, the Peace Corps, the Public Health Service, the U.S. Coast Guard, the U.S. Fish and Wildlife Service, and the U.S. Geological Survey.

An image from a NASA satellite reveals the huge size of Hurricane Irene as it makes landfall on the East Coast as a Category 1 hurricane in 2011.

JOB REQUIREMENTS AND COMPENSATION

Most government jobs in meteorology and atmospheric science require at least a bachelor's degree. Research positions are likely to require an advanced degree. Federal positions in meteorology involve a broad range of different work environments. Depending on the job description, a meteorologist may spend the day behind a desk, in a lab, or out in the field. Job seekers should read the job description closely to make sure that it fits their interests, aptitude, experience, and educational background.

Departments within the federal government list jobs on the Web site USAJobs.com. Federal employees are paid according to a fixed general schedule. Many government departments also offer student internships, both paid and unpaid. Volunteer

Officers with the 19th Weather Expeditionary Squadron install a weather sensor in a remote Afghan mountain pass. The sensor will provide weather data to the armed forces, as well as to the local population.

opportunities are also available for students interested in gaining experience in the field.

Meteorologists with the U.S. military include both civilian workers and service members on active duty, both officer and enlisted. Civilian meteorologists, who are hired through USAJobs.com, may be required to obtain top-secret clearance in order to work for the military. Soldiers who specialize in meteorology may enter the service with expertise in the field or may complete a training course upon enlisting. A weather specialist with the Air Force Weather Agency, for example, completes eight months of technical training after basic training. No previous educational experience is required, but the recruit should have a high school degree or the equivalent and an interest in science, computers, and technology. The recruiter may be able to inform the applicant in advance whether or not he or she is likely to be accepted into training as a weather specialist.

Applicants to the U.S. military must meet certain physical, aptitude, and educational requirements. They must also be willing to commit to a certain period of service. In addition to the skills and abilities required for meteorology—such as an interest in science and an attention to detail—members of the military must also have the qualities necessary for military service, such as personal discipline and a willingness to obey orders. Members of the military are paid according to grade and years in service. They also receive free housing and board and benefits.

chapter 4

CAREERS IN BROADCAST METEOROLOGY

Though not large in number, broadcast meteorologists are the most visible representatives in the field. People look to their local TV meteorologist—or the celebrity meteorologists on the Weather Channel and the national networks' morning news programs—for clear and informed explanations of the weather. Even off camera, however, most broadcast meteorologists are professionals with solid backgrounds in atmospheric science and experience in producing an accurate forecast. They are not just "weather readers."

WORKING FOR THE WEATHER DEPARTMENT

A TV station typically employs three to six meteorologists, depending on the size of the market it serves. A small TV station might employ a single meteorologist; large metropolitan areas have bigger staffs. A beginning meteorologist will generally start out in smaller markets, often working undesirable early morning or weekend hours. This will provide important on-the-job training for career advancement. He or she will gain experience and, perhaps, the opportunity to acquire credentials such as American Meteorological Society certification. The meteorologist can then move up to more a prominent and better-paying job at a bigger station. A broadcast meteorology career may require moving frequently, though sometimes meteorologists are promoted up the ladder within a TV station.

There are no formal educational requirements for being a broadcast meteorologist. Some weather forecasters have little understanding of the science behind the weather and merely pass on the NWS forecast or a forecast prepared by a consulting meteorologist working for a private company. Nonetheless, most TV stations require that applicants hold a degree in meteorology. There are also no absolute requirements for a background in communications, though some colleges offer majors specifically in broadcast meteorology. Many atmospheric science or meteorology majors who hope for a career in broadcast meteorology also take classes in communications.

A broadcast meteorologist's responsibilities extend beyond his or her work at the TV station. Many TV stations have

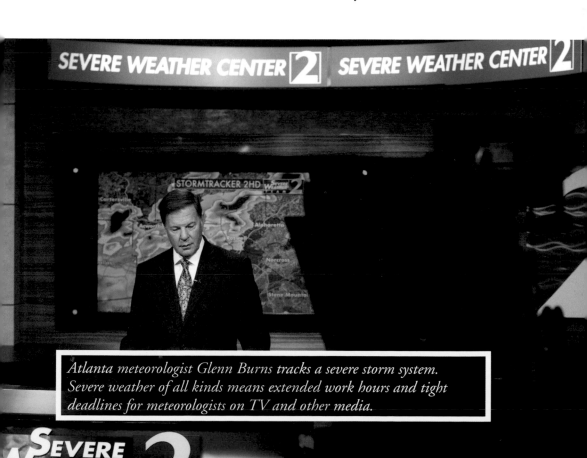

Atlanta meteorologist Glenn Burns tracks a severe storm system. Severe weather of all kinds means extended work hours and tight deadlines for meteorologists on TV and other media.

partnerships with newspapers and radio stations. Broadcast meteorologists may prepare the weather report for the local newspaper. They may record weather announcements for a local radio station. A broadcast meteorologist may keep a weather

Al Roker, weather anchor on NBC's Today *program, promotes a charitable effort. Now a well-known entertainment personality, Roker got his start in TV while still finishing his college degree.*

blog on the TV station's Web site and contribute material for online publication. Viewers may send e-mails with questions or comments, or send in their own weather photos. Meteorologists generally respond to such e-mails and participate in social media.

In addition, broadcast meteorologists may make public appearances around the area or do public service work in the community. In what little spare time they have, some meteorologists may also conduct research on specific topics in atmospheric science in order to improve forecasts and better understand weather patterns.

A DAY ON THE JOB

Before going on-air, a broadcast meteorologist compiles a number of different forecast models. The raw data for these models is provided by satellites, weather balloons, aircraft, weather buoys, ships, and weather stations around the world. All of this information is transmitted to World Meteorological Centers worldwide, one of which is in Washington, D.C. The data is then transferred to the National Centers for Environmental Prediction (NCEP), where it is analyzed by a highly advanced computer modeling tool called the Advanced Weather Interactive Processing System (AWIPS).

The results are sent to regional NWS Weather Forecast Offices, which produce forecasts tailored to their particular regions. The NWS then sends several different forecasts, which vary according to whether they are long-range or short-range, to the meteorologists at TV stations. Broadcast meteorologists may also consult more localized forecasts provided by private meteorological firms or nearby universities.

PROFILE: TOM SKILLING

Tom Skilling is one of the most recognizable broadcast meteorologists in the United States. He is the chief meteorologist for WGN-TV in Chicago, where he has worked since 1978. He also writes the "Ask Tom Why" weather column for the *Chicago Tribune*.

Skilling began his career in radio at the age of fourteen in Aurora, Illinois, while still in high school. In 1970, he began studying meteorology at the University of Wisconsin–Madison while continuing his work in radio and television. After graduating, he began working as a meteorologist for WITI-TV in Milwaukee, Wisconsin, in 1975. There, he was rated as the city's top meteorologist before moving to Chicago.

Skilling is known for his in-depth reports, his enthusiasm, and his innovative use of technology. In early 2004, he helped coordinate the Tribune Weather Center, which combines in one centralized location the meteorology resources of the *Chicago Tribune*, WGN-TV, and CLTV. The center includes a computer graphics system that meteorologists can use to track weather details across the Chicago metropolitan area.

The broadcast meteorologist consults these forecasts in preparing his or her own forecast. Sometimes the various forecasts largely coincide. Other times, there is much variation among the predictions, and the meteorologist must decide whether to go with a particular forecast or create a composite. In such cases, experience with local weather is hugely helpful. After a couple of years on the job, a meteorologist learns to recognize weather patterns in his or her broadcast area. Some meteorologists then create their own maps and graphics on the computer for the broadcast. Others have their graphics provided by private meteorological companies.

Once the camera is on, the meteorologist's work is to convey the weather forecast clearly to the audience. Viewers react most positively to a poised and competent weathercaster with an appealing TV personality and good delivery skills.

THE WEATHER CHANNEL

For many broadcast meteorologists, their dream job is working for the Weather Channel, the most visible and high-profile nation-wide employer of meteorologists. Since its first broadcast in 1982, the Weather Channel has transformed the weather forecast from a dry presentation to popular entertainment. During severe weather events, the channel brings experts into the studio to discuss the situation and sends meteorologists out into the field to shoot live footage. A job with the Weather Channel provides exposure to an audience of millions.

The Weather Channel began as a twenty-four-hour-a-day cable channel devoted exclusively to weather reporting and analy-sis. It then expanded to radio and the Internet. It now covers the entire country, providing both national coverage and six local fore-casts every hour, as well as international reporting. The Weather Channel is based in Atlanta, Georgia, and has offices in other cities across the country.

The Weather Channel proclaims itself a great place to work, citing its job benefits, work environment, and two-time inclusion on the "Top 10 Places to Work in Cable" list. Its Weather.com Web site lists job openings, which include internship opportunities.

JOB REQUIREMENTS AND COMPENSATION

Although a relevant degree is not absolutely necessary, most employers of broadcast meteorologists require or prefer candidates with at least a bachelor's in meteorology, broadcast meteorology, atmospheric science, or a related science major. Course work in communications and related extracurricular activities, such as participation in college television or radio, provide good experience

Florida resident Suzanne **Bonner***, who has experienced several hurricanes and seen her home ravaged, rises daily at 5 AM for the Weather Channel's "Tropical Update."*

for the job. Many TV stations and other media outlets hire interns. Employers are also likely to be impressed by internships or employment in other areas of the field—a NWS internship, for example. Broadcast meteorology can be highly competitive, and job seekers should look for ways to gain a solid background in the field.

A broadcast meteorologist must possess skills and abilities required for meteorology—such as an aptitude for science and an attention to detail—as well as excellent communication skills, both verbal and written. He or she must connect with the audience and interact well with colleagues at the station. This includes other broadcasters, management, and technical staff. Broadcast meteorologists should also be comfortable working with computers and high-tech equipment. Some employers prefer that candidates be familiar with camera equipment and be able to shoot video from the field.

Recent meteorology graduates might consider joining organizations such as the American Meteorological Society and the National Weather Association. These professional groups offer opportunities for job searches, networking, and professional guidance. The American Meteorological Society offers a certified broadcast meteorologist rating,

Weather Channel meteorologist Vivian Brown delivers the forecast. In the studio, the meteorologist actually stands in front of a blank screen; the maps are added to the video in postproduction.

which replaced an earlier "seal of approval" designation.

Job seekers must submit an audition tape along with other application materials. Recording the video requires access to a TV studio. Many candidates prepare their tape as a part of broadcast meteorology course work in college or during internships at TV weather departments. Established meteorologists are paid well, and a few top broadcasters in major metropolitan areas earn celebrity-level salaries. Starting out, however, a broadcast meteorologist usually does not earn much more than minimum wage.

chapter 5

OTHER PRIVATE-SECTOR METEOROLOGY CAREERS

The private sector is a huge area of growth within the field of meteorology. Modern technology is constantly improving the accuracy and precision of forecasts. Faster computers and more sophisticated models mean that meteorologists can issue forecasts and predict trends that address specific weather niches. For example, farmers, insurance companies, and airplane pilots all require highly accurate weather forecasts for their livelihoods, but the specific focus will be different for each forecast. Private consulting meteorologists can address their client's particular requirements.

Another significant private-sector area is environmental meteorology. Instead of issuing forecasts, environmental meteorologists examine how weather impacts the environment and how both, in turn, affect human welfare and enterprises. They also study how pollution affects the atmosphere, weather, and environment. Some environmental meteorologists are employed by government agencies, such as the EPA and NASA. Others work in the private sector for environmental organizations and a variety of private industries.

The list of potential clients for both consulting meteorologists and environmental meteorologists is extensive.

Examples include companies involved in commerce, agriculture, fisheries, construction, transport (especially aviation), utilities, emergency management, finance, and insurance. All of these industries have a stake in knowing how short-term weather events

Modern meteorology can provide farmers with tailored forecasts that provide precise information on weather patterns for a specific geographic area.

and long-term weather patterns will affect their businesses. Such application of private-sector meteorology is sometimes referred to as "industrial meteorology" or "information services."

A meteorological forecast of severe weather may cause a pilot to change a flight plan in order to avoid any risk of dangerous flying conditions.

METEOROLOGY CONSULTING FIRMS

Like NWS meteorologists and broadcast meteorologists, consulting meteorologists begin by analyzing weather forecasts issued nationally and fine-tuning the results. In some cases, the work of consulting meteorologists is very similar to that of other meteorologists, and they may serve the same clients. Media outlets and private industries often receive meteorological information from a variety of sources. A TV station that consults NWS forecasts and employs its own meteorologists may also have a contract with a private meteorology consulting firm. An airline may use forecasts issued by both the NWS and private firms. Some airlines even have their own meteorology departments.

Consulting meteorologists can provide highly specific forecasts for clients who are dependent on specific aspects of the weather. For example, a consulting meteorologist might prepare a snow forecast for a small town that would be more detailed than the NWS or TV station forecast. City managers would use these highly localized and specialized forecasts as they make crucial decisions regarding school closures or the deployment of snowplows and salting trucks. A ski resort would use the forecasts to anticipate the length and quality of the upcoming ski season and allocate their resources accordingly. The forecasts would help them determine which runs to open and how much artificial snow-making would be required, as well as likely revenue for the season.

Consulting meteorologists also work for sports and recreation clients. They might issue forecasts for beach resorts, golf courses, and baseball parks—all enterprises whose operations and profits depend upon fair weather. Utility companies hire consulting meteorologists to prepare forecasts regarding how upcoming weather might affect the need for services. People require more electricity during a hot spell in the summer, for example, and use

Wade Stettner, official on-site meteorologist of the PGA (Professional Golfers' Association) Tour, is charged with making weather decisions that keep golfers and spectators safe.

more heating gas during a cold spell in the winter, and utility companies need to be prepared for these surges in customer demand and energy usage. Consulting meteorologists also prepare forecasts relating to agriculture, which are used by farmers as well as commodity traders whose profits depend on the correct anticipation of future prices for crops.

Even the legal system has a high demand for the services of consulting meteorologists. Law firms and insurance companies frequently require meteorological expertise. Some of these companies keep consulting meteorologists on staff, while others hire the services of meteorology consulting firms for specific cases. Much of the work involves forensic meteorology, in which the consulting meteorologist reconstructs past weather conditions based on meteorological records. A consulting

FORENSIC METEOROLOGY

Forensic scientists piece together evidence in order to get a clear idea of how an event unfolded. The practice is used to figure out how accidents occurred and crimes were committed. Forensics can cover a broad range of sciences and specialized fields, including meteorology.

Forensic meteorologists use a variety of techniques to recreate weather conditions. They begin by collecting standard weather information, such as temperature and wind speed, for the day, time, and location of the event being investigated. They may also gather data from specialized sources that can pinpoint phenomena such as lightning strikes or hailstorms. In addition to looking at meteorological records, they may also go to the scene of the event and proceed to interview eyewitnesses.

Forensic meteorologists summarize their findings in reports and sometimes give evidence in court. They may put together computer model presentations to demonstrate weather conditions at the time and location of an incident as an accompaniment to their testimony.

meteorologist may be asked to determine whether icy roads could have contributed to a car accident, whether a windstorm was the likely cause of property damage, or even how weather conditions could have affected a crime scene. A consulting meteorologist's conclusions can be central to determining the outcome of a lawsuit, insurance settlement, or environmental regulatory action.

ENVIRONMENTAL METEOROLOGY FIRMS

The field of environmental meteorology became a significant employer of meteorologists with the passage of the Clean Air Act and subsequent amendments, especially the regulations mandated in 1970. Overwhelming research had shown the damaging effects of pollution on human health and the environment, and the government took action. Environmental meteorologists were involved in drafting the legislation. As a result of the new pollution control laws, the demand increased for environmental work related to air quality.

These environmental meteorologists monitor air quality, measure air pollution, conduct research, and test emissions of factories and other polluters. They may record their findings in an environmental impact statement intended to force a polluter to curb emissions. In other cases, environmental meteorologists are tasked with determining the potential impact of a new plant being built or an existing facility being expanded. They create models of how the pollution will be dispersed into the atmosphere. Environmental meteorologists also test and monitor ozone levels and track the pollutants that predict ozone levels so that the public can be informed when the air quality becomes dangerous.

In addition to air quality work, environmental meteorologists study broader connections between weather, climate, and

A researcher adjusts equipment on a small weather station set up for an experiment monitoring the effects of ozone on plants and soil organisms.

the environment. While forecast meteorologists can predict the weather over relatively short periods of time, environmental meteorologists can use meteorological tools and historical data to analyze larger trends in climate variability.

JOB REQUIREMENTS AND COMPENSATION

All meteorology careers require a strong background in science, math, and computers. Most meteorology jobs call for a bachelor's degree in a relevant major. Meteorologists who run their own company or hope to work in management may benefit from taking business courses or earning MBA degrees.

The American Meteorological Society offers a certified consulting meteorologist designation. In order to qualify, meteorologists must hold a degree, pass a written test, and submit to a work review. Achieving certified consulting meteorologist status demonstrates a high level of professional competence to potential employers.

Meteorology jobs in the private sector encompass a variety of responsibilities, daily routines, and work environments. An air quality meteorologist may spend extended periods of time in the field. A forensic meteorologist may be required to testify in court, so he or she must be prepared to present facts and answers to questions clearly and succinctly, at a level a layperson can understand. An environmental meteorologist must be familiar with various federal and state environmental laws. Both consulting and environmental meteorologists may have to deal with more paperwork than forecast meteorologists.

Pay and benefits also vary greatly. Unlike government or broadcast jobs, private sector meteorological work does not always offer a clear career arc in terms of advancement and pay raises.

chapter 6

ACADEMIC AND RESEARCH CAREERS IN METEOROLOGY

Aspiring meteorologists with a passion for discovery, lifelong learning, and keen intellectual curiosity might be most drawn to academic and research careers in meteorology. Research and teaching jobs often intersect with other career fields within meteorology. For example, a prominent broadcast meteorologist might teach classes at a nearby college. NWS forecast meteorologists often pursue research in addition to their regular duties. A researcher might do consulting work on the side. Most educators and researchers, however, hold advanced degrees.

Over a hundred universities and colleges across the country offer degree programs in atmospheric science and related sciences, and many more offer coursework in meteorology. They employ thousands of meteorologists as teachers and offer research opportunities.

TEACHING METEOROLOGY

The principle responsibility of meteorology professors at colleges and universities is to teach their craft to students in the classroom. Some schools may employ a single professor to teach a few meteorology classes. Schools with substantial atmospheric science programs may employ a large meteorology faculty that teach classes ranging from introductory meteorology to specialized seminars for graduate students. No matter the size of the program, professors prepare lesson plans, hold office hours, grade student work, and serve as student advisers.

Faculty members also conduct research and oversee graduate, and sometimes even undergraduate, student research. Research projects are often sponsored by government or private grants. Some faculty and students may pursue research supported by the University Corporation for Atmospheric Research, a consortium of over seventy-five North American colleges and universities that offer doctorates in atmospheric and related sciences. Funded by the National Science Foundation, UCAR promotes research in topics ranging from high-altitude observation of the atmosphere to air-sea interactions.

University and college professors are sometimes under intense pressure to publish their research findings in journals or books. For a younger associate professor, publishing one's work increases the chances of receiving a promotion to full tenured professorship. It also adds to the department's prestige.

A professor points out features on a projection of a weather map during a lecture to a meteorology class.

In addition to teaching and research, university and college professors perform various duties for their department. They attend department meetings and serve on committees addressing topics such as curriculum requirements.

Meteorology degree holders with a passion for teaching may also choose to teach in community colleges or at the high school or elementary school level. Community college instructors take on many of the same types of responsibilities as university professors, but they are less likely to be given research opportunities. Teachers at elementary and high schools will probably teach general natural science courses that might include meteorology as a unit. Education and experience in meteorology provide a good background for teaching science at any level.

METEOROLOGICAL RESEARCH

Most research in meteorology is supported by government agencies. The agencies that make up the National Centers for Environmental Prediction conduct research related to forecasting and modeling. The National Oceanic and Atmospheric Administration operates a separate branch that sponsors research on topics related to climate, oceans, coasts, lakes, weather, and air quality. The national laboratories run by the Department of Energy are some of the nation's leading research institutions, and some of them offer opportunities in atmospheric research. Various other government agencies, including the Environmental Protection Agency, the Department of Agriculture, NASA, and the Department of Defense, conduct research related to their core missions. State and local governments also support research work.

A great deal of research is conducted at universities and other educational institutions. Yet private research groups and industries also support research and development related to weather, atmosphere, and climate. Many successful research projects are joint ventures among government, academic, and

A researcher launches a radiosonde weather balloon carrying a package of instruments that collects weather data. When the balloon bursts, the instruments return to Earth by parachute.

private organizations. The University Corporation for Atmospheric Research manages the National Center for Atmospheric Research, a leading atmospheric research facility, which is also supported by the private sector. According to the magazine *Science*, NCAR research covers "weather prediction and forecasting, severe-storm physics, pollution and air chemistry, global warming, interactions between the Sun and the Earth, and the impacts of weather on society including everything from agriculture to national security."

Atmospheric research is conducted in a variety of settings. The researcher may spend most of his or her time in the field or at a computer. Lab work will also be likely, since some research attempts to reproduce atmospheric conditions in a controlled setting in order to understand physical and chemical properties and processes. Scientists generally specialize in either applied research or basic research. Applied research deals with observing, analyzing, and forecasting weather and climate. Basic research attempts to increase the fundamental knowledge of atmospheric processes related to weather. In the end, the common goal of much research related to meteorology is to better understand how the atmosphere works and improve weather and climate predictions.

Atmospheric researchers often work as part of a multidisciplinary team that might also include chemists, physicists, climatologists, hydrologists, oceanographers, engineers, computer programmers, or mathematicians. Each member will bring his or her expertise to complex weather topics that involve multiple branches of science.

JOB REQUIREMENTS AND COMPENSATION

Advanced degrees—a master's and Ph.D.—in meteorology, atmospheric science, or a related subject are essential for

STORM CHASERS

Howling winds, looming funnel clouds, and speeding along bumpy backcountry roads are all part of the job description for storm chasers, who have one of the most action-packed jobs in meteorology. Storm chasers are severe weather specialists who pursue tornadoes and gather data about them using video, photography, radar, and a variety of high-tech tools that measure wind speed and direction, air temperature, and humidity. Their goal is to help scientists understand how and why tornadoes form.

Storm chasers may work for universities, research facilities, or media outlets. They work mostly in the Midwest, where more tornadoes are reported than in any other part of the United States. They spend much of their time out in the field, waiting for reports of storm formation and then driving to find them in specialized vehicles equipped to gather storm data. A storm-chasing trip might last for several days without a single storm sighting.

When a tornado is spotted, storm chasers move quickly to catch up so that they can observe as much of the storm as possible. Approaching a tornado is extremely dangerous. Storm chasers face hazards that range from high winds and lightening strikes to falling debris and car accidents. They may have to scramble to get out of the way of a storm if it suddenly changes direction. Professional storm chasers emphasize that this is a very dangerous undertaking that should be left to trained and experienced experts.

advancement as a researcher or a professor at a college or university. Good college grades and relevant experience, such as internships, can help gain admittance into top graduate school programs. Students in master's or doctorate programs may assist faculty as teaching assistants, which provides a great opportunity to gain teaching experience.

A professional storm chaser gets close to a tornado, acquiring breath-taking footage and contributing to the scientific understanding of severe weather.

College or university professors generally start out as assistant professors and rise to become associate professors and then full professors. Faculty members work to gain tenure at their institution, which guarantees them a permanent position. For faculty members with tenure, teaching at a college or university is a very secure, well-paying job with good benefits. Researchers employed by the government are paid according to a fixed general schedule, which ranks pay rate into fifteen different grades. A highly educated atmospheric scientist would probably be ranked in one of the higher pay levels.

chapter 7

RELATED CAREERS

Meteorology is closely related to several other environmental sciences. Instead of a dedicated and independent department for meteorology, many colleges and universities have a department of atmospheric and oceanic sciences or a school of geographical sciences that covers multiple disciplines, including meteorology, under one umbrella. The study of the atmosphere and weather is closely related to the study of the oceans, climate, and water cycle, and all of these sciences depend on the basic laws of chemistry and physics.

A career in these fields requires many of the same interests and aptitudes that are essential for meteorology. All natural scientists must have great curiosity for how the physical world works, as well as proficiency in science, math, and computers. Some scientists work in subfields where two branches of science intersect, such as hydrometeorology or atmospheric chemistry.

In addition, science writers and editors and public policy experts bring the work performed by scientists to the attention of the public. Instrument designers, hardware manufacturers, and software engineers produce the tools and equipment that make meteorological work possible.

CLIMATOLOGY

Climatology is the study of average weather over long periods of time—thirty years or more. Like meteorology, climatology is

NOAA incident meteorologists (IMETs) are dispatched in the field during critical weather situations. Here, an IMET sets up a weather station near an Idaho wildfire.

a branch of atmospheric science. The difference between the fields is that meteorology focuses on short-term forecasts, while climatology deals with a much longer time frame.

Climatologists study weather data from the past to develop climate models and make climate pattern predictions. They draw on a wide variety of sources of information. Climatologists studying fairly recent climate history consult data, such as temperature, rainfall, and wind, collected from the same types of sources used by meteorologists—satellites, radar, and weather stations. Climatologists studying weather patterns going back hundreds, thousands, or tens of thousands of years consult historical records, study archaeological evidence, examine rings on ancient trees, and analyze samples taken from ice cores. Their research reveals the causes and consequences of climate change over time.

The effects of climate change are relevant to every branch of natural science, however, not just climatology. Atmospheric scientists, meteorologists, and experts in other disciplines all conduct research on climate change, what causes it, what its effects are, and how to cope with its worst consequences.

OCEANOGRAPHY

Oceanography is the study of the ocean, comprising physical oceanography, chemical oceanography, biological oceanography, and geological oceanography. Physical oceanography examines physical conditions, from waves, currents, and tides to temperature and salinity (salt levels). This branch also considers the interactions of the ocean with the land, seafloor, and atmosphere, and the ocean's connections with weather and climate.

Oceanographers may work "in the field"— on research vessels or along ocean coastlines.

They also work in labs and behind computers—like atmospheric scientists, oceanographers create models to try to understand and predict natural processes. Oceanographers obtain their data from buoys, instruments on board ships, and

Legendary oceanographer Sylvia Earle, a National Geographic explorer-in-residence, examines a patch of sargassum, a seaweed that provides habitat for marine wildlife.

satellites. Satellite technology, in particular, provides valuable, globe-spanning information about oceans.

In addition to oceanography, a couple of other branches of natural science study water. Inland, limnologists study bodies of fresh water, including lakes, ponds, rivers, streams, and wetlands. Hydrologists study the distribution of water in the environment. They work in water conservation, forecast water conditions such as flooding and drought, and monitor water quality.

PHYSICS AND CHEMISTRY

The field of physics examines the basic principles and laws that apply to the motion, energy, structure, and interactions of matter. The field of chemistry also examines matter and energy, but chemistry focuses more on transformations of matter, such as through chemical reactions. Both disciplines can be applied to atmospheric science.

Atmospheric physicists use their knowledge of physics to examine processes such as cloud formation, heating and cooling in the atmosphere, and atmospheric electricity. Atmospheric chemists investigate topics such as the chemical makeup of the atmosphere and the interactions of the various components of the atmosphere. Both atmospheric physicists and chemists work with other types of scientists to model various processes in the atmosphere and study broader topics such as climate change, the impact of pollution, and ocean-atmosphere interactions.

Other specialized branches within atmospheric science include aeronomy, which is the study of the upper atmosphere, and dynamic meteorology, which is the study of the motions of the atmosphere. Physical geography is the broad field of earth science that examines the physical characteristics of Earth.

TIPS FROM THE EXPERTS

When asked to give advice to young, aspiring meteorologists, nearly all the professionals in the field emphasize the importance of a strong background in science and math. They acknowledge that students might be drawn to the field by the excitement of severe weather situations or the glamour of being on television, but they always emphasize that the job requires years of serious and disciplined study involving math and science.

Professionals also tend to find that students are unaware that meteorology is such a broad field. Beyond forecasting and broadcast meteorology, there are many opportunities in the private sector, particularly among organizations and industries that are not primarily devoted to weather-related issues. Young people should explore all the possibilities of the field when considering a meteorology career.

Meteorology is a field that is constantly advancing, as computers become more powerful and models become more complex. It's a good idea for a meteorologist to continue learning throughout his or her career in order to keep up-to-date on new developments regarding techniques, research, and instruments. The American Meteorological Society and other organizations periodically offer seminars and conferences to help working meteorologists stay current.

METEOROLOGY TECHNOLOGY

Meteorologists are supported by the people who work with the instruments that gather data and who help ensure that the weather forecasts reach their audience. Meteorological instrument design is a small but crucial niche within the field of industrial design. These instruments are complex, highly

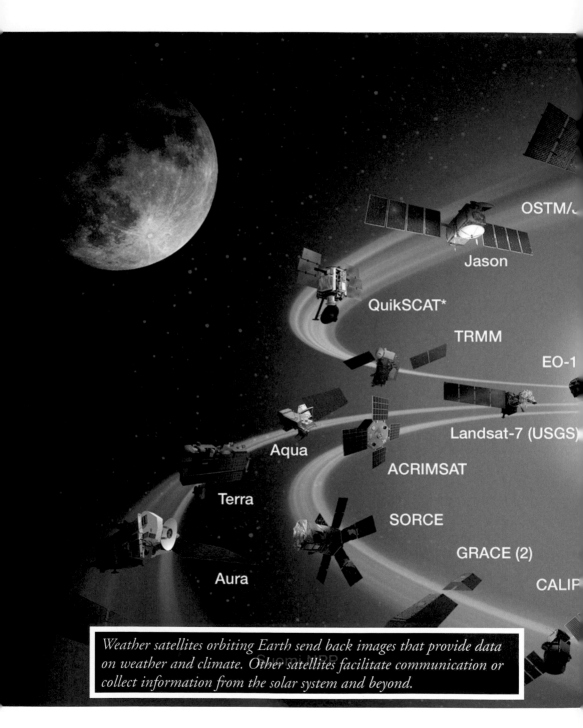

OSTM/J

Jason

QuikSCAT*

TRMM

EO-1

Landsat-7 (USGS)

Aqua

ACRIMSAT

Terra

SORCE

GRACE (2)

Aura

CALIP

Weather satellites orbiting Earth send back images that provide data on weather and climate. Other satellites facilitate communication or collect information from the solar system and beyond.

Aquarius

AA)

CloudSat

specialized, and—in some cases, such as with weather satellites—unique. Meteorology requires a huge range of instruments that measure weather phenomena—from rainfall and humidity to the height of clouds—with precision and accuracy. Meteorological instruments are often manufactured by large high-tech corporations.

Equipment technicians play an important role in maintaining instruments. They install, service, test, and repair equipment ranging from thermometers and weather station instruments to Doppler radar systems. Technicians consult with meteorologists and other scientists and, in some cases, with the designers and manufacturers of meteorological equipment. Meteorologists are also supported by computer experts who work with hardware and software.

WRITING, EDITING, AND POLICY

Science writers produce articles, reports, books, and other

written pieces on topics related to science, including weather, climate, and atmospheric science. Their audience ranges from the general public to specialists in the field being addressed. A science writer has the responsibility of conveying complex technical information accurately, yet also on a level that will be comprehensible to the specific audience. A science writing assignment may require extensive research that might include interviewing experts. Some science writers work as public information officers (also called public relations or communications staffers) for organizations such as universities, museums, government agencies, and nonprofit organizations. Science editors prepare the material for publication and oversee the overall publishing process.

Policy experts are scientists with experience and training relevant to shaping legislation and regulations related to their field. A policy expert in atmospheric science might help draft reports on climate change or emergency preparedness for weather events such as hurricanes. Policy experts might work for politicians or for scientific organizations that can provide unbiased information on a subject. They are also employed by industries and environmental groups that lobby for a specific agenda.

JOB REQUIREMENTS AND COMPENSATION

Job requirements, responsibilities, and pay for the various careers related to meteorology vary greatly. More information for each can be found in the Bureau of Labor Statistics' *Occupational Outlook Handbook*. Like meteorologists, natural scientists in related fields often work for the government, universities, or private industries. Most jobs require a bachelor's degree, and research positions require a graduate degree.

A meteorological instrument designer is recommended to have at least a bachelor's degree in industrial design or a related major. A job in instrument design requires attention to detail, computer proficiency, and problem solving skills. A meteorological equipment technician should have an associate degree in instrumentation technology or a related program. A technician should possess mechanical aptitude, the ability to work under pressure, and good communication skills. Many meteorological instrument technicians work for the companies that manufacture the equipment.

Many science writers and editors have education and experience in science, as well as skills in research and writing. Often, science writers work as freelancers and produce pieces on a variety of topics, although they may specialize in a specific area.

glossary

aviation The designing, building, or operating of aircraft.

buoy A float anchored to the bottom of a body of water.

civilian Nonmilitary.

climatology The study of the climate.

drought An extended period of abnormally dry weather.

forecast An analysis and report of expected future weather conditions.

humidity The amount of water vapor in the air.

hydrology The study of the waters of Earth and atmosphere.

meteorology The science and study of the atmosphere and its phenomena.

oceanography The study of the ocean.

precipitation Any form of water that falls from the clouds to Earth's surface.

radar Acronym for "radio detection and ranging"; an instrument that detects characteristics of distant objects by how they reflect radio waves.

satellite An object that revolves around a celestial body; weather satellites are equipped with instruments that collect weather data.

solar flare A sudden eruption on the surface of the sun that can disrupt communications systems and other technology on Earth.

water cycle The circulation of water in any state throughout Earth, atmosphere, and bodies of water.

weather balloon A type of high-altitude balloon that transmits weather data during its flight from an instrument called a radiosonde attached to the balloon.

for more information

American Meteorological Society (AMS)
45 Beacon Street
Boston, MA 02108
(617) 227-2425
Web site: http://www.ametsoc.org
The AMS is the premier professional organization of meteo-
    rologists. It promotes education in the field, offers
    certification, and provides career and job information.

Canadian Meteorological and Oceanographic Society (CMOS)
P.O. Box 3211, Station D
Ottawa, ON K1P 6H7
Canada
(613) 990-0300
Web site: http://www.cmos.ca
The CMOS exists for the advancement of meteorology and
    oceanography in Canada.

Environment Canada—Weather and Meteorology
Inquiry Centre
10 Wellington, 23rd Floor
Gatineau, QC K1A 0H3
Canada
(819) 997-2800
Web site: http://www.ec.gc.ca
Environment Canada, which operates the Meteorological
    Service of Canada, issues regular weather forecasts and
    severe weather warnings, in addition to providing
    Canadians with a variety of specialized products and
    services that enable people to make their weather-
    related decisions sooner and with greater confidence.

National Atmospheric and Oceanic Administration (NOAA)
1401 Constitution Avenue NW, Room 5128
Washington, DC 20230
Web site: http://www.noaa.gov
The NOAA is the government agency that studies and pre-
    dicts changes in climate, weather, oceans, and coasts. It
    also manages coastal and marine ecosystems.

National Weather Association (NWA)
228 West Millbrook Road
Raleigh, NC 27609
(919) 845-1546
Web site: http://www.nwas.org
The NWA is a professional organization of operational
    meteorologists.

National Weather Service (NWS)
1325 East West Highway
Silver Spring, MD 20910
Web site: http://www.nws.noaa.gov
A NOAA agency, the NWS provides weather, hydrologic, and
    climate forecasts and warnings for the United States, its
    territories, and adjacent water and ocean areas.

University Corporation for Atmospheric Research (UCAR)
Mesa Laboratory & Visitor Center
Mesa Lab & Fleischmann Building
1850 Table Mesa Drive
Boulder, CO 80305
(303) 497-1000
Web site: http://www2.ucar.edu
A nonprofit consortium of seventy-five North American
    Universities, the UCAR serves as a hub for research, edu-
    cation, and public outreach for the atmospheric and

related earth sciences community. It also manages the National Center for Atmospheric Research (NCAR).

World Meteorological Organization (WMO)
7bis, avenue de la Paix
Case postale No. 2300, CH-1211
Geneva 2, Switzerland
Tel.: + 41(0)22 7308111
Web site: http://www.wmo.int
A specialized agency of the United Nations, the WMO coordinates international efforts pertaining to the state and behavior of Earth's atmosphere, its interaction with the oceans, the climate it produces, and the resulting distribution of water resources.

WEB SITES

Due to the changing nature of Internet links, Rosen Publishing has developed an online list of Web sites related to the subject of this book. This site is updated regularly. Please use this link to access the list:

http://www.rosenlinks.com/ECAR/Meteo

for further reading

Aguado, Edward, and James E. Burt. *Understanding Weather and Climate*. 5th ed. Upper Saddle River, NJ: Prentice Hall, 2009.

Ahrens, C. Donald. *Meteorology Today: An Introduction to Weather, Climate, and the Environment*. 9th ed. Florence, KY: Brooks Cole, 2008.

Allaby, Michael. *Encyclopedia of Weather and Climate*. New York, NY: Facts On File, 2007.

Dunlop, Storm. *Guide to Weather Forecasting*. Buffalo, NY: Firefly Books, 2010.

Ferguson Publishing. *Discovering Careers for Your Future: Environment*. New York, NY: Ferguson, 2008.

Fleisher, Paul. *Doppler Radar, Satellites, and Computer Models: The Science of Weather Forecasting*. Minneapolis, MN: Lerner Publications, 2011.

Fry, Juliane L., et al. *The Encyclopedia of Weather and Climate Change: A Complete Visual Guide*. Berkeley, CA: University of California Press, 2010.

Gaffney, Timothy N. *Storm Scientist: Careers Chasing Severe Weather*. Berkeley Heights, NJ: Enslow, 2009.

Mogil, Michael. *Extreme Weather: Understanding the Science of Hurricanes, Tornadoes, Floods, Heat Waves, Snow Storms, Global Warming, and Other Atmospheric Disturbances*. New York, NY: Black Dog and Levanthal Publishers, 2007.

Yeager, Paul. *Weather Whys: Facts, Myths, and Oddities*. New York, NY: A Perigee Book, 2010.

bibliography

American Meteorological Society. "Career Center: All About Careers in the Atmospheric and Related Sciences." Retrieved February 2012 (http://www.ametsoc.org/careercenter/careers.html).

Bell, Trudy E. *Science 101: Weather.* Irvington, NY: Collins, 2007.

Bureau of Labor Statistics. *Occupational Outlook Handbook.* Washington, DC: U.S. Department of Labor, 2011.

Department of Defense. "Department of Defense Weather Programs." Retrieved March 2012 (http://www.ofcm. gov/fedplan/fp-fy09/pdf/3Sec3c-DOD.pdf).

DiClaudio, Dennis. *Man vs. Weather: Be Your Own Weatherman.* New York, NY: Penguin Books, 2008.

Ferguson Publishing. *Careers in Focus: Meterology.* New York, NY: Ferguson, 2011.

Fox, Tom. "National Weather Service Director Jack Hayes on His Organization's Atmosphere." *Washington Post,* June 29, 2011. Retrieved February 2012 (http://www. washingtonpost.com/blogs/ask-the-fedcoach/post/ national-weather-service-director-jack-hayes-on-his- organizations-atmosphere/2011/03/04/ AG3MflqH_blog.html).

Hile, Kevin *The Handy Weather Answer Book.* 2nd ed. Detroit, MI: Visible Ink Press, 2009.

National Weather Service Forecast Office. *Careers in Meteorology: Job Information for Those Interested in Meteorology.* San Diego, CA: National Weather Serive Forecast Office, 2006.

NOAA. "Biographies: Dr. John L. 'Jack' Hayes." November 18, 2011. Retrieved February 2012 (http://www.nws.noaa.gov/com/presentations/hayes.htm).

NOAA. "Jetstream—Online School for Weather." Retrieved February 2012 (http://www.srh.noaa.gov/jetstream/nws/nws_intro.htm).

Reynolds, Ross. *Guide to Weather*. Buffalo, NY: Firefly Books, 2005.

WGNTV. "Tom Skilling, WGN Chief Meteorologist." 2012. Retrieved February 2012 (http://www.wgntv.com/wgntv-storm-chase-bio-skilling,0,647449.story).

Williams, Jack. *The AMS Weather Book: The Ultimate Guide to America's Weather*. Chicago, IL: University of Chicago Press, 2009.

index

A

Advanced Weather Interactive
  Processing System, 37
Air Force Weather Agency, 20, 28, 33
American Meteorological Society,
  11, 14, 34, 41, 52, 65
anemometer, 30
apprenticeships, 12
associate degree, 10–12, 69
astronomy, 14
Aviation Weather Center, 21, 22

B

bachelor's degree, 12–14
barometer, 30
broadcast meteorology, 5, 10, 11,
  14, 34–43, 47, 52, 53
Bureau of Land Management, 31
Bureau of Reclamation, 31

C

Center Weather Service Units, 19
chemistry, 9, 13, 60, 64
Climate Prediction Center, 21
climatology, 14, 60–62
college and university education, 5,
  11, 12–14, 20, 26, 32, 35, 38,
  40–41, 43, 52, 53–55, 57–58,
  60, 68–69

community college, 10–12, 55
computer science, 13–14, 23
Cooperative Program for
  Operational Meteorology,
  Education, and Training, 11

D

Defense Meteorological Satellite
  Program, 29
Department of Commerce, 17
Department of Energy, 29, 55

E

earth sciences, 9, 64
electronics, 12
engineering, 12
environmental meteorology firms,
  44–46, 50–52
Environmental Modeling Center, 21
Environmental Protection Agency,
  30, 44, 55
extracurricular activities, as career
  prep, 9, 40

F

Federal Emergency Management
  Agency, 25
financial aid, 10, 14
forecasting, do-it-yourself, 30

ABOUT THE AUTHOR

Corona Brezina has written numerous books on science and technology careers, including careers in nanotechnology, sustainable energy, and medical examining, as well as titles devoted to economics, the environment, and job skills. She lives in Chicago, Illinois.

PHOTO CREDITS

Cover (meteorologist) © iStockphoto.com/Mike Cherir; cover (background), p. 1 Melanie Metz/Shutterstock.com; back cover © iStockphoto.com/blackred; pp. 4, 31 Getty Images; pp. 6–7, 42–43 Bloomberg via Getty Images; p. 9 Hill Street Studios/Blend Images/Getty Images; p. 12–13 Katie Deits/ Photolibrary/ Getty Images; pp. 18–19 Joe Raedle/Getty Images; pp. 22–23 Jim Edds/ Photo Researchers/Getty Images; pp. 24–25 David Hay Jones/Photo Researchers, Inc.; p. 28 Michael Nagle/Getty Images; p. 32 U.S. Air Force Weather Agency photo by Army Sgt. 1st Class Luis Saavedra; p. 35 T. Lynne Pixley/The New York Times/Redux; pp. 36–37, 40–41 © AP Images; pp. 44–45 Goodluz/Shutterstock.com; pp. 46–47 Carlos E. Santa Maria/Shutterstock.com; p. 48 Chris Condon/US PGA Tour/Getty Images; p. 51 Simon Fraser/Photo Researchers, Inc.; p. 54 © Bob Mahoney/The Image Works; p. 56 Chris Sattlberger/Photo Researchers, Inc,; p. 59 Carsten Peter/National Geographic Image Collection/ Getty Images; p. 61 NOAA.gov; pp. 62–63 Shaul Schwarz/ Getty Images; pp. 66–67 NASA; back cover © iStockphoto .com/blackred

Designer: Matt Cauli; Photo Researcher: Marty Levick